3260

THE CLARINETIST

Classic Pieces for Clarinet & Piano

Music Minus One

SUGGESTIONS FOR USING THIS MMO EDITION

WE HAVE TRIED to create a product that will provide you an easy way to learn and perform concerted pieces with a full accompaniment in the comfort of your own home. Because it involves a fixed performance, there is an inherent lack of flexibility in tempo. The following MMO features and techniques will reduce these inflexibilities and help you maximize the effectiveness of the MMO practice and performance system:

Where the soloist begins a piece or movement *solo*, we have provided subtle introductory taps, inserted at the actual tempo, before the soloist's entrance.

We have observed generally accepted tempi, but some may wish to perform at a different tempo, or to slow down or speed up the accompaniment for practice purposes. You can purchase from MMO specialized CD players & recorders that allow variable speed while maintaining proper pitch. This is an indispensable tool for the serious musician and you may wish to look into purchasing this useful piece of equipment for full enjoyment of all your MMO editions.

We want to provide you with the most useful practice and performance accompaniments possible. If you have any suggestions for improving the MMO system, please feel free to contact us. You can reach us by e-mail at *mmogroup@musicminusonecom*.

Music Minus One

3260

CONTENTS

<table>
<tr><td colspan="2">DISC A
COMPLETE
VERSION
TRACK</td><td>DISC B
MINUS
VERSION
TRACK</td><td></td><td>PAGE</td></tr>
<tr><td></td><td></td><td>1</td><td>Tuning Notes</td><td></td></tr>
<tr><td></td><td>1</td><td>2</td><td>Stamitz: Concerto No. 3 – Theme from 2nd Movement (Romanze)</td><td>4</td></tr>
<tr><td></td><td>2</td><td>3</td><td>Mozart: Divertimento No. 1, KV439b – Minuet & Trio</td><td>5</td></tr>
<tr><td></td><td>3</td><td>4</td><td>Mozart: Divertimento No. 2, KV439b – Minuet & Trio</td><td>6</td></tr>
<tr><td></td><td>4</td><td>5</td><td>Mozart: Divertimento No. 3, KV439b – Rondo</td><td>8</td></tr>
<tr><td></td><td>5</td><td>6</td><td>Mozart: Divertimento No. 5, KV439b – Minuet, Trio</td><td>10</td></tr>
<tr><td></td><td>6</td><td>7</td><td>Mozart: Divertimento No. 5, KV439b – Adagio</td><td>11</td></tr>
<tr><td></td><td>7</td><td>8</td><td>Beethoven: Duo No. 2, WoO 27 – Rondo</td><td>12</td></tr>
<tr><td></td><td>8</td><td>9</td><td>Beethoven: Duo No. 2, WoO 27 – Aria</td><td>13</td></tr>
<tr><td></td><td>9</td><td>10</td><td>Beethoven: Duo No. 3, WoO 27 – Theme</td><td>14</td></tr>
<tr><td></td><td>10</td><td>11</td><td>Spohr: Andante, op. 34</td><td>15</td></tr>
<tr><td></td><td>11</td><td>12</td><td>Weber: Variations for Clarinet and Piano, op. 33: Theme</td><td>16</td></tr>
<tr><td></td><td>12</td><td>13</td><td>Weber: Grand Quintetto, op. 34: Theme from 2nd Movement</td><td>17</td></tr>
<tr><td></td><td>13</td><td>14</td><td>Weber: Concerto No. 2, op. 74: Theme from 2nd Movement (Romanze)</td><td>18</td></tr>
<tr><td></td><td>14</td><td>15</td><td>Weber: Concerto No. 1, op. 73: Theme from 2nd Movement – Adagio ma non troppo</td><td>19</td></tr>
<tr><td></td><td>15</td><td>16</td><td>Weber: Andante, Theme and Variation, op. posth.</td><td>20</td></tr>
<tr><td></td><td>16</td><td>17</td><td>Schubert: The Shepherd on the Rock, op. 129</td><td>21</td></tr>
<tr><td></td><td>17</td><td>18</td><td>Mendelssohn: Concert-Piece No. 2, op. 114: 2nd Movement</td><td>22</td></tr>
<tr><td></td><td>18</td><td>19</td><td>Mendelssohn: Concert-Piece No.1, op. 113: 2nd movement</td><td>24</td></tr>
<tr><td></td><td>19</td><td>20</td><td>Goldmark: Rustic Wedding Symphony, op. 26</td><td>26</td></tr>
<tr><td></td><td>20</td><td>21</td><td>Schumann: Fantasie-Stück, op. 73</td><td>27</td></tr>
<tr><td></td><td>21</td><td>22</td><td>Schubert: Octet: Solo from 2nd Movement – Andante un poco molto</td><td>28</td></tr>
<tr><td></td><td>22</td><td>23</td><td>Brahms: Symphony No. 3: Solo from 2nd Movement – Andante</td><td>29</td></tr>
<tr><td></td><td>23</td><td>24</td><td>Brahms: Symphony No. 4: solo from 2nd Movement – Andante moderato</td><td>30</td></tr>
<tr><td></td><td>24</td><td>25</td><td>Rimsky-Korsakov: Concerto for Clarinet and Band – Andante</td><td>31</td></tr>
</table>

Concerto No. 3
for Clarinet and Orchestra
Theme from Second Movement (Romanze)

4 taps (1 measure)
precede music

Karl Stamitz

Divertimento No.1
Minuet and Trio

3 loud/ 2 soft taps
precede music.
Clarinet strts on 1st soft tap.

Wolfgang Amadeus Mozart, KV439b

Menuetto D.C.

MMO 3260

Divertimento No.2
for Two Clarinets and Bassoon
Minuet and Trio

5 taps plus 1 silent tap
precedes music.
Start on silent beat.

Wolfgang Amadeus Mozart, KV439b

Tempo di menuetto (♩=116)

Trio

Menuetto D.C.

Divertimento No.3
Fifth Movement (Rondo)

4 taps (2 measures)
precede music

Wolfgang Amadeus Mozart, KV439b

Divertimento No.5
for Two Clarinets and Bassoon
Minuet, Trio and Adagio

5 taps (1²/3 meas.)
precede music

Wolfgang Amadeus Mozart, KV439b

Duo No.2
for Clarinet and Bassoon

Rondo

3 taps (1½ measures)
precede music

Ludwig van Beethoven, WoO 27

Allegro moderato (♩=76)

Duo No.2
for Clarinet and Bassoon
Aria

5 taps plus 1 silent
($1^2/3$ meas.) precede music

Ludwig van Beethoven, WoO 27

Duo No. 3
for Clarinet and Bassoon
Theme

3 taps plus 1 silent
(¾ meas.) precede music

Ludwig van Beethoven, WoO 27

Andantino con moto (♪=100)

cresc. poco a poco

Andante
for Clarinet and Strings

4 taps (1 measure)
precede music

Louis Spohr, op. 34

Variations for Clarinet and Piano

Theme

4 taps (1 measure)
precede music

Carl Maria von Weber, op. 33

Grand Quintetto

for Clarinet and Strings
Theme from Second Movement (Fantasia)

Carl Maria von Weber, op. 34

Concerto No. 2
for Clarinet and Orchestra
Theme from Second Movement (Romanze)

Carl Maria von Weber, op. 74

Concerto No. 1 for Clarinet and Orchestra
Theme from Second Movement

Carl Maria von Weber, Op. 73

Andante, Theme and Variations
for Clarinet and Strings
Theme and Variation I

3 taps plus 1 silent
(¾ meas.) precede music

Carl Maria von Weber, op. posth.

The Shepherd On The Rock
Clarinet Solo from Song for Soprano, Clarinet and Piano

Franz Schubert, op. 129

Concert Piece No.2

for Clarinet, Basset Horn and Piano
Second Movement

Felix Mendelssohn-Bartholdy, op. 114

Concert Piece No.1

for Clarinet, Basset Horn and Piano

Second Movement

Felix Mendelssohn-Bartholdy, op. 113

Rustic Wedding Symphony
Solo from Fourth Movement (In The Garden)

Carl Goldmark, op. 26

Fantasiestück (Fantasy - Piece)
for Clarinet and Piano

Robert Schumann, op. 73

Delicatamente e con espressione

Octet
Solo from Second Movement

6 taps (1 measure)
precede music

Franz Schubert, op. 166

Andante un poco molto (♪=92)

Symphony No. 3
Solo from Second Movement

4 taps (1 measure)
precede music

Johannes Brahms, op. 90

Symphony No. 4
Solo from Second Movement

Johannes Brahms, op. 98

Concerto for Clarinet and Band

Andante

Nikolai Rimsky-Korsakov

MUSIC MINUS ONE
50 Executive Boulevard
Elmsford, New York 10523-1325
800-669-7464 (U.S.)/914-592-1188 (International)

www.musicminusone.com
e-mail: mmogroup@musicminusone.com